Looking Aft
Number

Six plays about the

Paul Groves
Head of English
St Hugh's Church of England Comprehensive School
Grantham

Nigel Grimshaw
Formerly Senior Lecturer in English
Kesteven College of Education
Peterborough

John Murray

Contents

First published 1984
by John Murray (Publishers) Ltd
50 Albemarle Street, London W1X 4BD

British Library Cataloguing in Publication Data

Groves, Paul
Looking after number one.
1. Readers—Drama
I. Title II. Grimshaw, Nigel
428.6′2 PE1127.D72

ISBN 0–7195–4121–2

Phototypesetting by Inforum Ltd, Portsmouth, Great Britain
Printed in Hong Kong by Wing King Tong Co Ltd

Looking After Number One

Jill (16)
Mum
Dad
Mr Masters, *the manager of Pennywise supermarket*
Vicky, **Dave**, **Dula** — *workers in the supermarket*

Scene 1

(Jill's House)

Jill Does this look all right, Mum?
Mum I'm sure it does.
Jill You don't think it's too much?
Mum No. You must look your best.
Jill I think I'll change it for the red one.
Mum Why? It's very nice.
Jill No, I'll change it. And then you can help me with my hair.
Mum You're not going for a fashion model's job, you know. It's only a supermarket.
Jill You don't really understand how hard it is to get a job. There'll be lots of other girls there. I must stand out.
Mum I do understand, dear. I'm not that stupid.
Jill I don't want to be on the dole for ever.
Mum I'm sure you won't be.
Dad *(coming in)* You off then?

Jill I'm just going to change this dress for the red one and then Mum's doing my hair.

Dad Well, don't be all day. Your interview's at eleven. I want to get some shopping done first.

Mum Just leave her, will you? Don't you panic her. There's plenty of time.

Dad There's a lot of traffic on Fridays.

Mum You'll be all right. Don't fuss!

Scene 2

(Pennywise supermarket office)

Mr Masters Come in, Miss Wilks.

Jill Thank you.

Mr Masters Take a seat.

Jill Thank you.

Mr Masters I've read your application. It was very neat. You'd be surprised at some of the rubbish I get. You have a good report from your school.

Jill I did my best.

Mr Masters And you've done well at Maths and English. That's not always the case.

Jill I liked English.

Mr Masters I've had people applying here who couldn't even read the *Beano*. They could hardly write their own names.

Jill Some of my friends had a lot of difficulty with reading and writing.

Mr Masters I don't know what schools are coming to. If I was as inefficient, I'd soon be out on my neck. Now, you would start off stacking the shelves. Infilling. There's always work to do. We like goods brought to the front of the shelves.

Jill Yes.

Mr Masters And there's these damned new 'sell-by' dates and regulations to make life more uncomfortable.

Jill My Mum always looks at the 'sell-by' date.

Mr Masters Don't they all? They all want the freshest. As if the rest wasn't fit to eat. Still, you'll get some cheap food as a member of staff if you come.

Jill Are there prospects?

Mr Masters That's a good question. The answer is – if you fit in. I like to think we're a happy team here. If you do well on the shelves we train you on the tills.

Jill And after that?

Mr Masters And after that, my dear, most young girls run off and get married. But if you can stick with us, the sky's the limit. Mrs Scott started on the shelves and now she's my assistant manager on a very good salary. Right, time is money. Go and see Mrs Scott. She'll give you details about pay and holidays. You'll know whether you've got the job by next Friday. Good day.

Jill Thank you very much.

Scene 3

(Jill's house. The following Friday)

Jill Has the postman come yet?

Mum No.

Dad He'll be here soon.

Jill I do hope he brings a letter from Pennywise.

Mum You mustn't be too disappointed if you don't get it.

Jill There were three other girls waiting.

Mum You said you thought you did well.

Jill I liked Mr Masters. He was really friendly. But I don't know . . .

Dad Here's the postman.

Jill I'll go.

(**Jill** *goes out*)

Mum I do hope something's come.

Dad Well, she seemed to have had a good interview.

Jill (*coming back*) A letter from Gran. Yes . . . no, it's two bills for Dad. There's nothing from Pennywise.

Mum Don't be upset, dear.

Jill I can't help it. I felt so sure Mr Masters wanted me.

Dad There'll be other jobs.

Jill There won't be.

(*The phone rings*)

Mum I'll go.

Dad I'll speak to Bob. He might find something with the Council.

Jill I'll never work. I know it.

Mum It's for you, Jill. A man.

(**Jill** *goes out*)

Dad She's very upset.

Mum I can't make her see reason.

Dad I mean, she's got a good home here. We can look after her.

Jill (*rushing in*) Mum! Dad! I've got the job!

Mum Oh, I'm so pleased, Jill.

Dad We must celebrate.

Scene 4

(*In the storeroom at Pennywise*)

Jill It's fun here, isn't it?

Vicky I wouldn't call it that.

Jill I mean I like the people so it doesn't seem like work.

Vicky They're not a bad bunch.

Dave Not bad. Could be worse.

Vicky Just push this rubbish skip outside, Jill.

Jill Righto.

Vicky The lorry comes this morning. Don't leave it.

Jill I won't.

Vicky Cover it first, Dave. We don't want any blowing about in the wind.

Dave I'll do just that.

Jill Oh dear, I've dropped my ear-ring in it.

Vicky I'll find it. Leave it to me.

Jill I can look.

Vicky I said leave it to me.

Jill There's some bacon in here.

Vicky Out-of-date stock.

Jill And some sides of meat.

Dave It's all rubbish, leave it.

Jill The date's all right. It's not rubbish.

Vicky Shall we tell her, Dave?

Dave We'd better.

Vicky We have a little arrangement with the driver of the lorry. You keep quiet and you'll get your cut.

Jill But it's stealing!

Vicky With the wages we get, the firm is stealing from us. This just gives us a proper wage. Are you with us?

Jill I don't want any part in it. I won't say anything but I don't want any part in it. I want to keep my job here.

Dave Look out, Masters is coming.

(**Mr Masters** *enters*)

Mr Masters Ah, Jill, I want you.

Jill Yes, Mr Masters.

Mr Masters You've been doing well here, Jill. I've been keeping an eye on you. I like your cheerful smile around the place. The customers like it, too. I'm putting you on the tills next week. Come and see Mrs Scott.

(**Mr Masters** *and* **Jill** *go out*)

Vicky Do you think she'll tell?

Dave She'd better not.

Scene 5

(On the tills in Pennywise)

Dula How are you getting on, love?

Jill All right.

Dula Nice to have a bit of a lull, isn't it?

Jill Yes, it can get hectic.

Dula Look, I wanted to see you. One or two 'friends' are in today.

Jill Friends?

Dula You know what I mean. Are you with us to do a bit of under-ringing?

Jill Under-ringing?

Dula You are green, aren't you?

Jill Green?

Dula Yes, when a 'friend' comes she'll put down a can of salmon first with a banker's card on it. Then you don't ring up the full price on her goods. You knock pounds off. And then we'll see you're all right at the end of the week.

Jill But that's dishonest.

Dula It's the world we live in. Are you with us?

Jill I want no part in it. I don't want to lose my job.

Dula Here's Masters. I'll see you later.

Scene 6

(Mr Masters' office, two weeks later)

Mr Masters Come in, Jill. Sit down.

Jill Thank you.

Mr Masters I can trust you, can't I?

Jill Oh yes, Mr Masters.

Mr Masters Well, I want you to tell me who's fiddling this firm.

Jill Fiddling?

Mr Masters Stealing. Tell me what you know.

Jill I don't know anything.

Mr Masters Come off it. That's one reason I put you on the tills so soon. There's so much stuff gone in the last quarter, everyone in the firm must know about it.

Jill They're all my friends. I can't say anything.

Mr Masters So you do know something.

Jill I didn't say that. You're getting me all confused.

Mr Masters Look, it's your afternoon off. I'll give you till tomorrow to think about it. Then, if there's no information, there's no job. You're out.

Jill It's not fair. I've worked so hard.

Mr Masters Business never has been fair. You've today to think about it.

Scene 7

(Jill's house)

Jill So what shall I do, Mum?

Mum You'll have to tell him.
Jill But they're my friends. I enjoy working with them.
Dad You've just got to think of your own skin.
Jill It's like telling tales at school.
Dad The world outside is tougher than school. You've got to look after number one, dear.
Jill I can't do it.
Mum If you don't tell, Mr Masters will think you are involved. I don't want your name in the paper.
Jill I don't know what to do.

Scene 8

(Mr Masters' office, next day)

Mr Masters Come in, Jill.
Jill Thank you.
Mr Masters Well?
Jill I've decided to tell you what I know.
Mr Masters I know it all, Jill. I had the CID in yesterday afternoon. I found some goods on the roof – I ask you! They caught Mrs Scott red-handed. She's coughed the lot. Do you know there were eight of them involved? What is the world coming to? I shall need evidence from you, of course. I'm glad you weren't in on it. There'll be promotion for you. I'll send for you later.

(**Jill** *goes out. The phone rings)*

Mr Masters Bodyglow Toiletries? Oh, yes. You want me to stock up well for Christmas? Sorry, mate, we're going to order a load of stuff from your competitors. What? Oh, yes. You're offering me a new car if I do. Be a bit obvious, wouldn't it? My wife? Oh no, I'm sure she wouldn't mind an early Christmas present. A little runabout, yes. No. No, don't come in tomorrow, I've had a load of stealing going on. I'll see you next week. It's a pleasure to do business with you.

People in the play

1 From what you have read in the play, what sort of person is Jill?
2 How does Jill's mother help Jill before the interview?
3 In which ways is Mr Masters what you might expect a boss to be?
4 What does Jill's Dad mean when he says, '. . . she's got a good home here. We can look after her'?
5 We do not meet Mrs Scott, but what sort of person do you imagine her to be?
6 Why do Dula, Vicky and Dave expect Jill to join in the stealing?
7 What do you think of Mr Masters when he puts pressure on Jill to help him stop the stealing?
8 What do you think of the advice Jill's parents give her about the stealing?
9 What does Mr Masters' last speech tell you about him?

First job

1 In which ways does Jill have the right idea about preparing for an interview?
2 What kind of qualities and qualifications does Mr Masters seem to want in persons applying for this job?
3 Should Maths and English be considered so important for this job in a supermarket?
4 Is it best to begin a job at the bottom in spite of any qualifications you might have?
5 Should you be yourself at interviews or put on a bit of an act?

Honesty at work

1 Vicky argues that they have to steal from the firm to make up for the poor wages they are paid. What do you think of her attitude?
2 How would you have reacted in Jill's situation?
3 Dula tells Jill that they cheat the firm because everybody does

it – 'It's the world we live in.' Is this true of this or other jobs? Is it true of the way people behave generally?

4 Who really pays for the stealing from supermarkets? Is it the manager, or the shareholders of the company owning the supermarket, or the people who shop there? Give some explanation for your point of view.

5 Is there any difference between what Mrs Scott has done and what Mr Masters does about Bodyglow Toiletries?

Writing

1 Newspaper headlines should be short, eye-catching and sensational. Write the headline for a newspaper account of what happens to Mrs Scott in court.

2 Describe how you would prepare for an interview, step by step. Number each sentence.

3 Look at the way this play is set out. Then write a scene for a play about what happens when Jill gets home and tells her parents that Mr Masters has found out about the stealing.

4 Dula's mother and father find out what Dula has been doing at work. They are upset about the publicity the court case will cause and what the neighbours will say. Write the scene for a play.

5 You are suspected of stealing but you know that the guilty person is a friend of yours. Write about what happens.

The Observers

The Tutor
Observer One
Observer Two
Observer Three
Observer Four
} *These can be either male or female characters*
Manager of the factory
Jack
Jim
Ted
Mick
Phil
Bill
Mick's wife

Scene

(The planet Zenyon. On a scanner, the Observers of planet Earth are about to see a town in the Midlands in Britain)

Observer One You say that on the Earth planet some people do not work?
Tutor That is correct.
Observer Two Are they ill?
Tutor No, they are not ill.
Observer Two I do not understand.
Tutor They have created a society where there is no work for some but there is for others.
Observer Three How odd.
Tutor We will look at Britain, a country in the northern hemisphere, and I will show you it is true.

Observer Three Then it is unfair. Do not those with no work revolt?

Tutor No. They are told it is necessary.

Observer Four I do not understand.

Tutor Let me show you on the scanner. We will look at an English town. It is a place of many factories.

Observer One But you told us that a factory is a place of work. You say there are many. I do not understand.

Tutor There is work in them for only some of the people. Let us look at this town. It is ten o'clock in their morning when the Sun star shines.

Observer One It is a pleasant town. Is that a factory?

Tutor That is the armaments factory. They make weapons there. Many people work there. They even work extra hours. But we are not looking there. Ah, here is our building.

Observer Two What are those tall orange things?

Tutor They are called cranes. They lift things for building work.

Observer Three Have they not discovered anti-gravity?

Tutor Not yet.

Observer Three How odd.

Tutor Look, there is a meeting of the work force in the canteen, an eating place. Look and listen. Here is the manager, the top man of the factory.

Manager I'm afraid there has been a downturn in the demand for our cranes because of the recession.

Observer Two What is a recession?

Tutor It means people are not trading with one another a great deal. People are not buying and selling.

Observer Four How odd.

Manager There seems no chance of an upturn in the immediate future. We must cut the workforce by 95. I am asking people from all departments to volunteer for redundancy by two o'clock this afternoon.

Tutor Redundancy means to give up your job because there is no work for you.

Observer Four Now, these unions you have told us about that look after the workers, won't they say, 'This is silly. No one should go. Work should be shared'?

Tutor No, they will not. They do not feel they have the power to do so when there are so few jobs.

Observer Well, what about these strikes you tell us about?

Tutor They do not think a strike would help.

Observer Four Why not?

Tutor They fear the management will shut down the factory and transfer the work elsewhere if they make trouble.

Observer One Workers and management do not work together, then?

Tutor No.

Observer One How odd.

Tutor Let us watch and listen to two workers talking.

Ted What are you going to do, Jim? You've been here 30 years.

Jim Maybe, but I can't afford to go. I still have my mortgage to pay off.

Observer Two What is a mortgage?

Tutor It is the money he owes for his house.

Observer Two He has to buy it?

Tutor Many workers do if they can.

Observer Two How odd.

Jim What about you?

Ted I'm only forty. There is a great shortage of jobs in this town for my trade. My wife could lose her job as well. I can't possibly volunteer.

Observer Four Is this happening at the armaments factory as well?

Tutor No, they have full employment. They have a full order book.

Observer Four For war they work; for peace they do not.

Observer Three How odd.

Tutor Yes, it is odd, but it is one of the things you must learn about the human race on the planet Earth.

Observer One What is going to happen at the crane factory? Will anyone volunteer not to work?

Tutor Let us move on to two o'clock. The Sun star is high in the sky.

Manager We have had just a handful of volunteers. I am afraid that now redundancy will become compulsory. During the afternoon you will be told if you have been selected. You will be paid redundancy money depending on your years of service. When you have been given your cards you must leave the factory within half an hour.

Observer One That man Jim has been there 30 years. Why must he leave so quickly? He must have friends he wants to say goodbye to. It is all so sudden.

Tutor The management feels that there might be trouble. They want it all over and done with quickly. Watch and listen further.

Manager Jack, here is a list of the redundant workers. First of all, go to the toolroom. All of them have got to go.

Jack All of them? The toolroom?

Manager Yes, but make sure you tell them one at a time. We don't want trouble. They're a bolshie lot.

Jack How can I?

Manager Find a way. Take them on one side or something. I'll see the office staff that have to go.

Jack I don't like doing this. Many of those men are my mates. I've worked with them for years.

Manager It's your job. You're paid to tell men what to do.

Jack This is the blackest day of my life.

Observer Three Is the manager afraid to face the men himself?

Tutor I think it is part of their class system. Bosses don't talk to shop floor workers. Let us now look at the scene in the toolroom.

Bill It's like waiting for a bomb to go off.

Phil They can't sack any of us. We're vital to the factory.

Bill I hope you're right.

Phil No, we must be safe in the toolroom.

Bill Hey up, here comes Jack.

Jack Sorry, Bill, you're first.

Bill What did I tell you, Phil?

Jack My heart sank when I saw your name, Bill.

Bill Who else here is on the list?

Jack I can't say.

Phil Here, give us that bloody list!

Jack Don't you assault me!

Phil We've a right to see that list.

Jack Get off!

Phil Got it. (*He reads it*) No wonder he didn't want us to see it. We're all on it.

Bill I said you couldn't trust them.

Jack It's not my fault. I just have a job to do.

Bill I wouldn't want to have your conscience, mate. Phil, you're the shop steward. What are we going to do about it?

Mick I've just finished my apprenticeship. What is the union going to do?

Phil That's just it. If we strike here they'll close down the whole factory and transfer the work to the other plant.

Mick They wouldn't dare.

Phil The other plant's a soft lot. The management have hinted several times that's what they'd do.

Mick Boss's dummies. This firm won't be satisfied until we're like Japanese workers, married to the firm.

Bill I don't think that would satisfy this lot. Is that all you've got to say, Phil?

Phil Sorry, mates. It's no different for me. But it could have been done in a better way, Jack.

Jack This is the worst day of my life.

Tutor Are you learning about the earth people?

Observer One It is unbelievable. Are they proud of their civilisation?

Tutor They think they are very advanced.

Observer Two It is so difficult to take in.

Tutor Let us follow one of the workmen home. We will go to Mick's house.

Mick's wife Redundant! Redundant! You can't be.

Mick I am, love.

Mick's wife But you've only just come out of your apprenticeship. You're twenty-one. We've bought this house on the strength of it.

Mick I'll get another job. You'll see.

Mick's wife With seventeen people out of every hundred out of work in the town?

Mick I'm a skilled man now. Something will turn up. There's your job to see us through.

Mick's wife But I want to have a baby. I want to give up work.

I've worked for the last three years.

Mick You'll have your baby.

Mick's wife I want a baby while I'm young.

Mick I'll go down to the Jobcentre in the morning. Don't take it like this, love.

Tutor Let us go back to the factory.

Jack There, I've done your dirty work for you. I never want to do anything like that again. Those blokes used to be my mates.

Manager You won't have to, Jack. I'm afraid I've just been handed this.

Jack Not my redundancy notice?

Manager Yes. Sorry, Jack.

Jack I can't believe you would do this.

Manager I'm sorry.

Jack You knew this all the time. You got me to do your dirty work and you knew all the time I was for the chop as well.

Manager It's only just come through.

Jack I helped to build this firm up. I helped to put it on its feet and you do this to me.

Manager You've been a great worker.

Jack See this grey hair. It's your firm that's caused this.

Observer One This cannot be true. I do not believe this is happening. You are tricking us.

Tutor No. It is happening.

Observer One I am glad I live on Zenyon then. What a barbarous place Earth is!

Tutor I can show you worse things about the planet Earth.

Observer Four I think we have had enough for one day.

Tutor Right. The lesson is finished.

People in the play

1 In what ways is the Tutor a good teacher?

2 What do we learn about the Observers themselves and their kind of world?

3 Is the Manager a hard man or does he have some sympathy for the workers? Give reasons for your answer.
4 How strong is the union at the factory? Is Phil, the Shop Steward, sensible or weak?
5 Who is the worst affected among the workers? Why do you think so?
6 Why are the toolroom workers so surprised at being made redundant?
7 Why is Jack's task so difficult?
8 How understanding is Mick's wife?
9 What upsets Jack most?

Redundancy

1 This play shows what can happen. Does anything surprise you about the way in which the workers were made redundant?
2 What might have been a better way of telling the workers that they were being made redundant?
3 There is a system for redundancy known as 'Last in, first out'. It means that people who have just joined a firm are the first to be made redundant. Those who have worked longer are in the next group of redundancies. Those who have worked longest are the last to be made redundant. What do you think of this system?
4 Why is there full employment at the armaments factory? Does this surprise you? Or do you think there should be full employment there?
5 What is 'work-sharing'? Would work-sharing help when orders are down and there isn't enough work in a factory? Is it a good idea?
6 Should a government try to create jobs, or should it let things take their natural course? Say why you think as you do.
7 Would a strike or a sit-in have helped with the situation in the play? Give reasons for your answer.
8 What sort of jobs do you think might disappear if the computer and the robot take over?

Writing

1 Look at the play again and then, in play form, write the scene of what happens in Mick's house the following day after he and his wife have had a sleepless night.

2 The Observers see a happier event on Earth, such as a wedding or a football match, which the Tutor explains to them. Write out what is said in play form.

3 You have a Saturday job. An older worker comes to you and says that his or her job is in danger because your boss is employing youngsters like you cheaply. Write the scene in play form.

4 Write a scene in play form in which the workers in this play plan a sit-in.

5 Write an account of what happens when Jack gets home.

6 Write an unrhymed poem called 'Mad Planet'.

Helpmates

Paul
Chris
Stephen
Penny
Shamin
Wendy
} *out-of-work teenagers*

Paul's Dad
Paul's Mum
Café owner (*female*)
Window cleaner (*male*)

Scene 1

(*A café*)

Paul Get me a tea, please.
Chris Right.
Paul Oh, here's Penny. Get her one as well.
Chris OK.
Paul Any luck?
Penny No. I think they really wanted a man. Kept asking me about boyfriends and if I wanted to get married.
Paul That's against the Sex Discrimination Act.
Penny Makes no difference. They still ask you.
Chris Two teas. Any luck?
Penny No.
Chris I wrote ten letters last week. One reply. I ask you – one reply. You'd think they'd have the manners to reply, wouldn't you?
Paul Yeh. So that's three of us on the dole.
Penny Five with Shamin and Wendy.

Chris Six with Stephen.

Paul Yeh. I don't think anybody I know really well is in work.

Penny I saw Shamin and Wendy at the Jobcentre with Steve. They said there was nothing on the boards. They'll be here in a minute. Oh, here they are.

Shamin Hello.

Paul Hello, Sha.

Stephen I'll get the teas.

Paul No luck, I hear.

Shamin No.

Wendy What do you expect?

Penny I've got an idea.

Paul What's this idea then, Penny?

Penny Well, I keep hearing people say that in spite of all this unemployment they can't get jobs done.

Paul So . . .

Penny So we form a group and do odd jobs.

Stephen What sort of jobs?

Penny Cutting grass.

Stephen That's only in the summer.

Penny Well, window cleaning and a bit of painting. Chris can mend lawn mowers.

Paul I put up that fence for my father.

Shamin I can hang wallpaper.

Penny I can type. I'm sure between us we've got a lot of talent.

Wendy We could do cleaning and babysitting.

Stephen What – the boys?

Wendy Why not?

Penny And we do it at a price people can afford. Until we get a lot of work. Then we can charge more.

Paul Do you mean we all work and share the profits?

Penny Yes, a co-operative. One of us would have to do the book work.

Wendy Who?

Penny I wouldn't mind.

Wendy Well, it's your brainwave.

Stephen What about taking work from skilled craftsmen?

Penny We don't take work from them. We only do work no one else wants.

Stephen And the unions?

Penny We would say that we were amateurs working for an amateur rate of pay.

Wendy You don't need a union to babysit.

Shamin You can get help if you set up your own business. I've seen a poster at the Jobcentre about it.

Chris Just a minute, before we all get excited about this. There's one thing we're forgetting.

Penny What?

Chris If we are self-employed, we lose our dole. And we have to pay our own National Insurance contributions.

Penny It's a risk worth taking. We can always go back on the dole if we fail.

Shamin We won't fail. It's a super idea.

Stephen I have my rent to pay. The rest of you live at home.

Penny We'll help you. That's the idea of a co-operative. We all help one another.

Paul I vote we give it a try.

Shamin Me too.

Penny I have other ideas as well. We take courses at college at night to get more skills. Later on someone might do a full-time course.

Chris Don't rush ahead. We'd have to get it off the ground first.

Wendy I'll give it a whirl.

Penny Steve?

Stephen OK. Count me in.

Penny Right. We need a name.

Stephen How about 'Help'?

Penny It sounds like the Samaritans.

Shamin You mean those people who stop people committing suicide?

Penny We don't want to get mixed up with them and we don't want people to think we are a charity.

Stephen It's difficult, all this thinking. I could do with a fag.

Chris Have this one.

Stephen But it's your last.

Chris This is a co-operative now. I don't want it.

Stephen Thanks, mate.

Wendy Perhaps you ought to give it up.

Penny Mate! That's it!

Shamin What?

Penny Helpmates.

Paul Great!

Shamin Brill.

Wendy That's a good name. Friendly.

Penny Now to the crunch. I want as much money as we can get together.

Stephen I thought this was to make money. We're not paying out, are we?

Penny We need to advertise in the local paper.

Stephen Can't we just advertise in shop windows?

Penny No, we want to look professional. So open your wallets and purses.

Chris Watch for the moths!

Café owner Are you lot going to stay here all day for six teas?

Chris We're unemployed, missis.

Café owner So will I be if I don't sell more tea.

Penny This is the sort of thing that makes me determined to succeed. We've got nowhere to go and we just get pushed around.

Chris We'll buy you out, missis, in a few months.

Café owner That'll be the day.

Scene 2

(Paul's house)

Paul's Dad I say no. You keep looking for a proper job. If you're off the dole, they won't bother about you.

Paul It's not fair. You've always had a job. You don't understand what it's like.

Paul's Dad I do.

Paul's Mum He's thinking about your future, Paul.

Paul So am I. But I've got to make my own future. Not like you. You had it made for you.

Paul's Mum That's not fair. Your Dad always worked hard to bring you up properly.

Paul I'm still going with the gang.

Paul's Dad Well, don't expect us to support you. Your bit of dole helps your Mum. I can't work for ever, you know.

Paul Some people would be glad to. Just let me go my own way.

Scene 3

(The café. One month later)

Penny Well, that's the end of our first week's work. After paying for National Insurance and so on, we have earned £5.20 each.

Shamin And all that babysitting I did!

Penny Well, you did have a job, Sha.

Chris I had three hours' work.

Paul I hated cleaning those windows. It was so cold.

Penny You'll get used to it. Steve's got a full week's work painting next week. We must help him with his rent, too.

Wendy So we really get less than £5.20.

Penny Yes.

Stephen Just a minute. I'm thinking of joining a pop group.

Penny Steve!

Stephen Well, I may as well be an unemployed pop star as earn five pounds a week.

Penny Stay with us for a bit, Steve, till we get off the ground. Can't you work with the group part-time?

Stephen I'll see.

Penny Give us a month.

Scene 4

(Paul's house)

Paul's Dad £5.20. You must be crazy.

Paul It'll pick up.

Paul's Mum My son a window cleaner. I always saw you in an office.

Paul I'll pick my own career, thank you. I'll do other jobs besides window cleaning.

Paul's Dad Well, I'm telling you to go back on the dole right away.
Paul No!
Paul's Dad Are you disobeying me?
Paul Yes.
Paul's Mum Oh, Paul.
Paul And I'm leaving home. Then you can't complain about supporting me.
Paul's Mum Paul, where will you go?
Paul I'm going to live with Steve.

(**Paul** *goes*)

Paul's Dad He'll be back. He can't live on five pounds a week.
Paul's Mum Oh, Paul!

Scene 5

(*The café. One week later*)

Penny At the end of the second week we have £8.05 each.
Paul That's a step in the right direction.
Shamin Babysitting all hours for that.
Penny Don't lose heart. Two of us have a full week's work lined up for next week.
Shamin Don't worry. I'll stick with you.
Penny Have you left home, Paul?
Paul Not yet. But I can't stand the atmosphere.
Penny What about your pop group, Steve?
Stephen I haven't decided yet.

Scene 6

(*The café. One week later*)

Penny I want to announce we have earned exactly as much as we would have done on the dole.
Shamin Yippee!
Wendy People are talking and telling each other about us.
Paul I did a simple plumbing job last week. I'm going to do an evening plumbing course at college.

Penny That's the idea. I expect your parents feel happier about that.

Paul Yeh. I shan't leave home for a bit in case Steve goes.

(**Window cleaner** *enters angrily*)

Window cleaner Hey, you kids!

Chris We're not kids.

Window cleaner You've pinched half my window cleaning round.

Chris We haven't pinched it. It's fair competition.

Window cleaner Nothing fair about your prices.

Chris And nothing fair about your window cleaning from what I've heard.

Window cleaner You cheeky young devil. I'll smash you.

Café owner OK. Out of here!

Window cleaner No.

Café owner I'll get the police.

Window cleaner You kids haven't heard the last of this.

(**Window cleaner** *goes off*)

Café owner Listen, he has a drink problem. Don't pinch his round. I know he doesn't do a very good job, but I expect he'll leave the district soon.

Penny OK. We don't want trouble. It's the first complaint we've had. We can do without the window cleaning.

Paul Thank goodness.

Café owner I must say I admire what you kids have done. It's free teas tonight provided . . .

Penny Provided what?

Café owner Provided one of you helps me out next week. I'll be short-handed.

Penny Leave it to Helpmates.

Wendy It's exciting, isn't it?

Shamin We're really going to make it. Does that mean we've got a full week's work next week?

Penny It does. I feel proud of you all.

Stephen Just a minute.

Penny What is it?

Stephen I've decided not to join the pop group full-time yet.

Penny Great, Steve.
Stephen I quite like being my own boss.
Paul My Mum's coming round to the idea so I needn't leave home.
Shamin Here's our tea. Let's drink a toast.
Penny To Helpmates.
Café owner To Helpmates.
All To Helpmates!

People in the play

1 Who is the driving force behind the Helpmates idea?
2 We know the reaction of Paul's parents, but have they any right to protest? Do you think any of the other parents might have objected?
3 Why does the café owner change her attitude?
4 Who might leave the group first? Give a reason for thinking as you do.
5 Who is least keen on the idea at first? Why do you think this?
6 Although they are united now they might start to split up. What could cause this?
7 Should bad workmen like the window cleaner be put out of business or sacked? Or has everyone the right to a job?
8 Paul does not like window cleaning. Should members of the group be allowed to choose their jobs, or should Penny decide what each one does?

Running your own firm

1 In a co-operative like this some people could work harder than others. How would you feel about this? Should the most skilful have more pay than the others?
2 Should the boys be paid more than the girls? Write down any arguments for or against.
3 Should Penny get more as she does the book work? Is she a kind of boss?
4 If your needs are greater, as Stephen's are – he has rent to pay – should you get more?

5 What would be the reaction to Helpmates from: (*a*) professional decorators and plumbers, (*b*) schoolchildren who babysit?

6 To get on in business do you have to be ruthless? Can you run a business successfully unless you are hard on your rivals and do your best to make them fail?

Writing

1 Write about two days in the life of one of the members of Helpmates: (*a*) a day before the scheme started, (*b*) a day at work.

2 Write down as a play the argument Paul's parents might have between themselves.

3 Write down as a play the scene where the group have just had their best week ever.

4 A newspaper uses the story of the group. Write down, complete with headline, the article or news item as it appears in the newspaper.

5 Write as a list any other things the group could do to earn money.

The Battle-Axe

Carol Lane
Miss Redman
David Foster, *a salesman*
Angie Smith, *a filing clerk*
Mr Lane } *Carol's mother and father*
Mrs Lane }
Mr Green, *manager of Porton Motors*

Scene 1

(The Sales Office of Porton Motors. **Angie Smith** *is putting some papers away in the filing cabinet.* **Miss Redman** *is speaking to* **Carol**, *who is sitting at her typewriter)*

Miss Redman You must get things right. I've told you that before.

Carol I'm sorry, Miss Redman. I couldn't quite read the writing on the worksheet.

Miss Redman It seems clear enough to me. Look – A.L. Walters & Co, not H.L. Walters. You really must be more careful.

Carol I'll try.

Miss Redman You'll have to do more than try. It's a simple enough job copying things out. There are hundreds of others who can do it, if you can't. Do it again.

(**Miss Redman** *puts a sheet of paper on the desk beside* **Carol** *and goes out)*

Carol (*types for a moment and then stops*) Is she ever in a good temper? I've been here two weeks now and she's been on at me every single day.

Angie Forget it. It's nearly home time. She's not perfect herself, you know.

Carol What do you mean?

Angie She forgets things. Loses things. I've heard Mr Green giving her a telling-off once or twice.

(**David Foster** *comes in*)

David What are you two nattering about?

Angie Miss Redman. She's been telling Carol off again.

Carol All I did was put an 'H' instead of an 'A' in an address. See, I've just typed it again.

David (*looks*) That's right. A.L. Walters. They're old customers. Everyone knows that.

Carol I didn't.

David You'll learn. Angie – Miss Redman's just given me the list of cars for sale for that advert of ours in the local paper. See it goes off tonight. (*He gives her the list*)

Angie Righto.

(**David Foster** *goes out*)

Carol (*types again and then stops*) That's the lot.

Angie How many are there?

Carol About fifteen.

Angie It's nearly time I was off. Do us a favour. Start sticking them in the envelopes while I do the post book.

Carol Okay.

(**Carol** *puts the invoices in their envelopes.* **Angie** *enters the addresses in the post book.* **Miss Redman** *comes in*)

Miss Redman Is that the post, Angie?

Angie Nearly finished, Miss Redman.

Miss Redman I'm afraid you haven't. There are a few more here that must go tonight. You'll have to wait until Carol has typed them.

Angie But I'll miss my bus, Miss Redman. I'll be ever so late home.

Miss Redman That can't be helped.

(**Miss Redman** *hands some papers to* **Carol** *and goes out*)

Angie What did I tell you? I'll bet she's been sitting on these all day and only just remembered them.

Carol I'll be as quick as I can. (*She starts typing again*)

(**David Foster** *comes in to look something up in a filing cabinet*)

Angie She's got no idea. She's a menace.

David Who's a menace?

Angie Miss Redman. She's got no consideration at all for anyone.

David Oh, no? Don't you know she devotes her whole life outside this office to looking after her invalid mother? Been doing it all by herself for years.

Angie Maybe. She's still got a mind like a sieve.

David That'll do. It's not up to you to go round criticising older members of staff.

Angie Well!

David That's enough.

(*He finds what he has been looking for in the filing cabinet and goes out*)

Angie There's a couple of good buses around now. Then there isn't another for an hour. How long will it take you to do the rest?

Carol I don't know. Half an hour. Maybe longer.

Angie Half an hour! I'll never make it. And I was going out tonight.

Carol Tell you what. Leave the stamps out and I'll post this last lot for you. You push off and get that bus.

Angie Smashing! I'll do the same for you one day.

(**Angie** *finishes entering the letters she has, puts on the last stamps and gets her coat*)

Angie 'Bye. Thanks a lot, Carol.

Carol Goodbye.

(**Angie** *goes out*)

Carol (*typing*) I'll be lucky to finish these in half an hour.

(*typing*) And what about my bus, eh? (*typing*) I'm fed up with this. (*typing*) I didn't think the job would be like this. (*typing*) And I'm more than just fed up with Miss Redman. (*typing*) Stupid old battle-axe.

Scene 2

(*The Lane's house.* **Mr Lane, Mrs Lane** *and* **Carol** *are sitting together*)

Mr Lane You're quiet tonight, Carol.
Carol Yes.
Mrs Lane And you were late back.
Carol That was Miss Redman. She came in with some stuff at the very last minute. I can't stand her.
Mr Lane The work's got to be done.
Carol She's always picking on me.
Mr Lane You're new. You've only been there two weeks. You've got to be told what to do.
Carol I wouldn't mind if it was only that. But she's really got it in for me.
Mrs Lane Perhaps she resents you because your Dad got you the job.
Carol I got the job myself.
Mr Lane Oh, yes? I suppose my asking Harry Slater to put in a word for you with your Mr Green had nothing to do with it.
Carol I wouldn't have got the job if I hadn't done well at the interview, would I? I've a good mind to pack it in.
Mrs Lane Don't be silly. Jobs are like gold dust these days.
Carol You don't know what it's like.
Mr Lane Don't we? I could tell you some tales about when I started. Some of the tricks we had played on us! Make your hair curl!
Carol She's not playing tricks. She's really got her knife into me, the old bag.
Mrs Lane You want to watch your tongue. Start talking like that in the office and you *will* be out of a job.
Carol Who cares?

Mrs Lane I care. I don't want you lounging about here at home day after day.

Carol Oh, what's the use?

(**Carol** *goes out*)

Scene 3

(*The office next morning. It is empty except for* **David Foster**. **Carol** *comes in quickly and hangs up her coat*)

David Good evening. Nice of you to find the time to come.

Carol I'm not all that late.

(**Angie** *comes in*)

Angie Hey, Carol – where did you put the post book last night?

Carol In the tray on top of the filing cabinet.

Angie It wasn't there when I got here this morning.

David Ask Miss Redman. She was here first.

(**David Foster** *goes out*)

Angie I had a smashing time last night. We went . . .

(**Miss Redman** *comes in*)

Angie Tell you later. I can't find the post book, Miss Redman.

Miss Redman I know. I've got it. You're late, Carol.

Carol I'm sorry, Miss Redman. My usual bus was full. I had to wait for the next.

Miss Redman Try for an earlier one tomorrow. Don't always leave things to the last minute.

Carol The earlier one gets me here just after eight.

Miss Redman Well, don't be late again. What happened to the post last night, Angie?

Angie Nothing, Miss Redman. I sent it off.

Miss Redman Why isn't it entered in the book, then?

Angie I did enter it.

Miss Redman Did you? I can remember at least five firms we sent post to. Their names are not in here. (*She holds up the* *book*) Unless . . . Carol, did you type those things I gave you just before you went home?

Carol Yes, of course.

Miss Redman Then why weren't they posted, Angie?

Carol They were posted. I posted them myself.

Miss Redman You posted them?

Angie She did it for me, Miss Redman. I had to get home.

Miss Redman I see. And was all that late post entered in the book?

Carol No.

Miss Redman Why not?

Carol I didn't think, Miss Redman. I was in a bit of a rush.

Angie It was my fault, Miss Redman. I didn't tell her.

Miss Redman She didn't need to be told. She ought to have known. I can't believe that anyone could be so stupid.

Carol I'm sorry, Miss Redman. I didn't think it was so important.

Miss Redman Of course it's important, you silly girl. This book is a record of all letters sent out.

Carol Yes, Miss Redman.

Miss Redman If a letter goes astray in the post, this book is proof that we sent it.

Carol It won't happen again.

Miss Redman It had better not. Don't try to do jobs that aren't yours.

Carol No, Miss Redman.

Miss Redman It's not good enough. I must say, if you go on like this, I can't see you lasting long in this job. Now – get on with your work.

(**Miss Redman** *goes out*)

Angie She's in a mood this morning, isn't she? Sorry I dropped you in it, Carol.

Carol (*starting to type*) She'd have soon found something to get at me about, anyway. Blast!

Angie What's up?

Carol (*tears the sheets out of her typewriter*) I've got something wrong already. The more she gets at me, the more mistakes I make.

Scene 4

(It is mid-morning in the office ten days later. **David Foster** *is loking something up in the phone book,* **Carol** *is typing and* **Angie** *is sorting papers for filing.* **Mr Green** *comes in. He is carrying a sheet of paper)*

Mr Green David! I've just had the *Gazette* on the phone. Haven't you sent them our advert this week?

David I haven't seen it, Mr Green. I imagine Miss Redman posted it off.

Mr Green Look in the post book, Angie. See when it was sent.

Angie Yes, Mr Green. (*She gets the post book and starts to look through it*)

Mr Green If you can't rely on the Post Office, who can you rely on?

David It's got to be at the *Gazette* today at the latest. Thursday's their print day.

Mr Green That's what makes it so annoying. Good thing they rang me.

David Yes. With trade this bad, we can't afford to miss a week's advertising. That *Gazette* advert usually pulls in some business.

Angie (*closing the book*) There's nothing been sent to the *Gazette* this week, Mr Green.

Mr Green Then where the hell is that advert? I know Miss Redman typed it out. I've got the carbon copy here. (*He shakes the sheet of paper he is holding*)

David Maybe Miss Redman's still got it. Where is she?

Mr Green She went out to replace a prescription she'd lost. Pills for her mother or something.

David Perhaps she lost the advert at the same time.

Mr Green Could be. I sometimes think she's getting past it.

David I'll ask her about it as soon as she comes in.

Mr Green Damn it! I don't want to stand about wondering where the thing might be!

Angie Shall we hunt around for it, Mr Green?

Mr Green Hunt around where?

David Wouldn't it be easiest just to send them a copy?

Mr Green Of course. Good thinking, David. Carol?

Carol Yes, Mr Green?

Mr Green I know I can rely on you to do a good job. Type a new copy of this. (*Gives her the sheet of paper*) And Angie . . .

Angie Yes, Mr Green?

Mr Green As soon as it's ready, stick it in an envelope and get it over to the *Gazette* right away. I'll ring them to tell them you're coming.

Angie Yes, Mr Green.

Mr Green See that Mr Wallace gets it. Mr Wallace in advertising.

Angie Mr Wallace. I won't forget.

Mr Green Good girl. David, come up to the office. There's a query on that Renault we took in last week.

David Right.

(**Mr Green** *and* **David** *go out*)

Angie Why me? It's always me.

Carol (*beginning to type the copy of the advert*) What's up now?

Angie Haven't you noticed? It's pouring outside. Chucking it down. I'll get wet through.

Carol Oh, hush. I don't want to make any mistakes with this.

Scene 5

(*The office some time later.* **Carol** *is alone until* **Angie** *comes in and takes off her wet coat*)

Angie What did I tell you? Look at me. That rain's ruined my hair. Ruined it!

Carol Poor old Ange.

Angie And now I'm behind with the filing. I'll have old Redman after me again.

Carol (*typing*) You had to go out. If your filing's not up to date, she can't complain.

Angie (*busy with the papers she is putting in order*) Oh, can't she? You wait. Where is she?

Carol She's just come back. I saw her pass the door. She must have gone upstairs to Mr Green.

Angie (*She takes the papers across to the filing cabinet, opens the top drawer and begins to file them away*) And they kept me hanging about at the *Gazette*. (*She is busy for a moment or two with the papers. Then she goes on*) They couldn't find that Mr Wallace. (*She finishes the top drawer, opens the second and stares into it*) What's this? (*She takes out a slip of paper*) Hey! I've found Miss Redman's prescription.

Carol Oh, good.

Angie And that's not all I've found. Well! The silly old bat! Look at this! And I had to go half way across town in pouring rain.

Carol What is it?

Angie It's the *Gazette* advert she typed. She must have dumped it here and forgotten it. And I'm soaked through.

Carol She was probably thinking of something else at the time.

Angie She hasn't got anything to think with. I'm going straight up to Mr Green with this to tell him about her.

Carol Don't do that.

Angie Why not?

Carol You'll get her into trouble.

Angie Serve her right. It's because of her I've had to run about in all that rain.

(**Miss Redman** *comes in*)

Miss Redman Is something wrong?

Carol Angie has found the prescription you lost, Miss Redman.

Miss Redman Oh? Thank you, Angie. Where was it?

Angie And that's not all I found. Look. Your advert for the *Gazette*. It was here in this drawer.

Miss Redman So that's where I left it. Oh dear! I must have been half asleep. Mr Green just told me it had been mislaid. He was quite annoyed.

Angie He would be, wouldn't he? I was going to take it up to him.

Carol There's no need for that.

Miss Redman Oh Lord above! It's having to sit up night after night with mother. You get so tired and irritable. So forgetful. (*She sits down*)

Carol I'd just drop it in the waste-paper basket.

Miss Redman (*She is thinking aloud and doesn't hear* **Carol**) I don't really think she'll live through the winter.

Angie Shall I do that, Miss Redman?

Miss Redman (*coming back to the present*) What?

Carol Let's throw it away. The advert is going in the *Gazette* now. There's no harm done.

Miss Redman You mean – not mention it to Mr Green?

Carol What good would it do?

Miss Redman Oh – that would be deceitful.

Angie She's just trying to keep you out of trouble, Miss Redman.

Miss Redman Oh – oh, I see. Well – thank you, Carol – but no. Give it to me, Angie. I'll just take it up to him and explain.

Angie Here you are. (*Gives her the advert*)

Miss Redman Thank you, Angie.

(**Miss Redman** *goes out*)

Angie I wouldn't have told him. Old fusspot.

Carol I suppose she has to – being Miss Redman. I feel a bit sorry for her.

Angie You won't when she starts getting at you again.

Carol I don't know. She must have a lot to put up with at home.

Angie True – and I bet there are worse people to work with than her. No job's perfect – that's what my Dad says.

Carol He could be right. The best thing to do is just to get on with it.

(*They both get down to work again and the play ends*)

People in the play

1 Is Miss Redman being fair to Carol at the beginning of the play? Say why you think as you do.

2 How do you know that Angie has been with the firm for some time?

3 Is David interested in Carol's problems with Miss Redman or not? How do you know?

4 How much sympathy does Miss Redman have for the problems and feelings of the two girls when she asks them to work late?
5 Do you agree with David when he says that they should not criticise older members of staff, or not? Explain your reasons for your answer.
6 Which of the people in the office seems to you the most considerate? Say why.
7 Why might Carol be very quiet when she gets home that night?
8 Which of Carol's parents seems more sympathetic to her problems? What makes you think so?
9 What evidence is there in Scene 3 that David can be sarcastic?
10 What evidence is there in Scene 3 that Angie is a bit frightened of Miss Redman?
11 In Scene 3 Miss Redman says that Carol ought to have known that all post should be entered in the post book. What can be said in defence of Carol?
12 Do you think Mr Green is a man who loses his temper easily or not? Give reasons for your answer.
13 What evidence is there that Mr Green doesn't think too highly of Miss Redman?
14 In Scene 5 how do you know that Angie is quite concerned about her appearance?
15 How can you tell that Miss Redman's mother must be quite old and ill?

Working conditions

1 Mr Green says that he knows he can rely on Carol to do a good job. Which do you think makes people work better, being praised for good work or knowing that they will be blamed for mistakes? Can you give some examples from your experience at home, school or work to support your views?
2 What are the sort of things you feel older people don't understand about younger people?
3 What do younger people often not understand about older people?

4 Carol offers to let Angie go to catch her bus and does some of Angie's work. But she is still angry about having to work late. Do you think Carol is too kind-hearted and a bit soft? Do you think her attitude at work is good or not? Do you think she will do well at the firm?
5 Do you think Angie's attitude to her work and other people is good or not? For instance, do you sympathise with her when she wants to get Miss Redman into trouble with Mr Green over the advert?
6 Do you think Miss Redman was right to report her mistake to Mr Green, or was Carol's idea of simply putting the advertisement into the waste-paper basket a more sensible one?

Writing

1 Is Miss Redman's mother a nice old lady or is she rather selfish and demanding? Write a scene in play form between Miss Redman and her mother when Miss Redman gets home at night.
2 How does Mr Green react when Miss Redman tells him how she lost the advert? Write the scene between them in play form.
3 By the end of the play Carol seems more settled in the job. Write a letter to a friend, as if you were Carol, saying what you think of Miss Redman and the job and how your feelings have changed.
4 Write your own story called 'First Day at Work'.
5 'I could see, right at that first moment, that he disliked me.' Use this opening sentence to write a story of your own about office life.

On the Dole

Neil Harper
Linda Harper, *Neil's wife*
Kath Banks, *Linda's sister*
Mrs Banks, *Linda's mother*
Andy Thomas
Greg Wilson

Scene 1

(The front room of the Harpers' house. **Neil** *is watching television.* **Andy** *and* **Greg** *put their heads round the door and come in)*

Andy No one home?
Neil Hello. Come in.
Greg We are in, mate.
Andy We couldn't make anyone hear by knocking. You were too wrapped up in that telly.
Greg Do you watch it all morning? What is it – Playschool?
Neil What else is there to do? Sit and think about being out of work?
Andy Come and do a bit with us.
Neil What?
Greg A bit of moonlighting, mate. Earn a bit on the side.
Neil Oh yes, and get nicked for it, eh? Didn't you hear what happened to Stan Slater?
Andy He was fool enough to get caught, wasn't he?
Neil What are you going to do?
Greg This and that. A bit of labouring.
Andy We could put you on our team.

Greg That's what we've come about.

Neil Not me, thanks.

Greg Where's Linda – and Nicky?

Neil Linda's out. Kath's taking Nicky for a walk.

Andy Linda's shopping, is she?

Neil Yes.

Greg Come off it, mate.

Neil Come off what?

Greg She's got a cleaning job at the Park Hotel, hasn't she?

Neil Who said?

Andy Mrs Clayton. She saw Linda going in there the other morning.

Neil That Mrs Clayton's a nosy, mouthy old bag. Don't spread it around, will you?

Greg Course not. Rely on us. We're just kidding.

Andy Still, if Linda can go out working on the side for a bit extra, why can't you?

Neil Linda doesn't have to go down for the dole. They don't know her so well.

Andy It doesn't make any difference.

Greg No. Go on – take a chance, mate. Help the black economy. Come and do a few jobs on the sly with us.

Neil Not me.

Andy Go on. It'll stop you sitting here brooding. You're in the house all the time. You haven't been in the White Swan for weeks.

Neil I don't go in there any more. I don't like their attitude.

Greg What attitude?

Neil All of them looking down their noses at me because I'm unemployed.

Andy You're imagining things. A lot of them who go in there are out of work, too.

Greg You're being soft. It doesn't bother me how they look at me.

Neil Well it wouldn't bother you, would it? Anyway, we're skint.

Andy Even with Linda's cleaning job?

Neil She doesn't get much. It's peanuts, really.

Greg All the more reason for coming with us.

Neil No thanks.

Andy Suit yourself. Don't say we didn't offer.

Neil No. Thanks a lot, anyway.

Greg Come on, Andy. We'd best be moving.

Andy Right.

(**Kath** *comes in*)

Andy Hello, Kath.

Greg And how's Linda's kid sister?

Kath All right, thanks.

Neil Where's Nicky?

Kath I left her outside. She wanted to play.

Neil You've not left her out at the front, have you? She could run into the road.

Kath She's out at the back and I've closed that little gate. She'll be all right.

Greg We're off. Cheers, mate.

Andy See you.

Neil Cheers.

Kath Bye-bye.

(**Andy** *and* **Greg** *go out*)

Kath What did they want?

Neil They're doing a bit of moonlighting. They wanted me to go with them.

Kath But you didn't.

Neil It's against the law, isn't it? If I was caught, I'd be for it. I'd be fined at least, maybe worse.

Kath Still – you really ought to do something. All you do is sit around all day. Or have another quarrel with Linda.

Neil Don't you start. I've tried. I've been after every job going. There just isn't any work anywhere. It's been over five months now.

Kath You could do something.

Neil What?

Kath Well, you can do free training at the Stadium. You can go swimming free any weekday at the baths in Freestone Street.

Neil Swimming? Don't be stupid.

Kath All right. You could go down to the College and take one of those courses. Then they've got a workshop you could use down at the Careers Centre.

Neil That's for kids.

Kath Well, you could try something. You look so miserable.

Neil Miserable! Of course I'm miserable. And I'm fed up to the back teeth with people telling me what to do.

Kath I was only trying to help.

Neil You're sticking your nose in! Leave me alone! I get enough of it from Linda. All I'm fit for nowadays is looking after a kid. For two pins I'd leave this house – and Linda and the kid – for good.

Kath I didn't mean any harm.

Neil Well, shut up, then! Just shut up!

Kath Right. I will. You can stew in your own juice. I promised Linda I'd do a bit of shopping for her. I'll go.

Neil Do that.

(**Mrs Banks** *comes in*)

Kath Oh, hello, Mum.

Mrs Banks Linda out at work, is she?

Neil Yes.

Kath I'm just off to do a bit of shopping for her.

Mrs Banks I see.

Kath I'll be back later.

Mrs Banks Right.

(**Kath** *goes out*)

Mrs Banks Why can't you do the shopping for our Linda?

Neil I wasn't asked.

Mrs Banks Too busy watching telly, I suppose.

Neil That's right. (*He switches it off*) I'm looking after Nicky.

Mrs Banks Are you? Where is she?

Neil Out at the back, playing.

Mrs Banks Have you been after any more jobs lately?

Neil No. What's the use?

Mrs Banks No use at all with that attitude, I'd say.

Neil Now don't start on that again. We've been through all that.

Mrs Banks I couldn't sit around day after day doing nothing.

Neil You just haven't any idea at all what things are like, have you? It gets you down after a while. You lose heart.

Mrs Banks I'd soon find myself a job.

Neil Talk sense. There aren't any jobs anywhere.

Mrs Banks Well, I'd do something. Look at this room.

Neil What's up with it?

Mrs Banks It's untidy. (*Goes to window and looks out*) And the garden. That's a mess, too. You could get a spade and dig it over. Plant a few vegetables.

Neil What do you want, anyway?

Mrs Banks What do you mean – what do I want? I've come to see Linda and Nicky. Where's Nicky? She isn't out here in the garden.

Neil She must be. Let's have a look. (*Goes to the window*) The little devil! She's on that old shed again. We've told her time after time not to climb up there.

Mrs Banks Oh! Look! She's going to fall!

Neil Quick! Come on!

(They both rush out)

Scene 2

(The same room some time later. **Neil** *is watching television again.* **Kath** *comes in)*

Kath Where's Mum? Gone?

Neil No, she's upstairs with Nicky. Nicky had a fall.

Kath Is she hurt?

Neil She cut her head. Nothing goes right, does it?

Kath And you've left it to Mum to look after her?

Neil She said I was getting in the way. It seems I can't even be trusted to put a plaster on my own kid these days.

Kath How did it happen?

Neil I wasn't keeping a proper eye on her, I suppose. Everything I touch goes wrong.

Kath And you love it, don't you?

Neil What?

Kath Feeling powerless. Being full of self-pity.

Neil What are you talking about? It was an accident.

Kath Look at you. You're young. You've got a nice wife in our Linda. You've got a lovely little kid. You're too wrapped up in yourself to care about either of them. All you can do is sit on your backside and moan.

Neil Oh, pack it in, will you!

Kath You're not ill. You're not dying. All you are is unemployed. There's millions in the same boat.

Neil And that makes it better, does it? You make me sick. You've no idea what it feels like to be out of a job and with no hope of getting one.

Kath Maybe not. But I know what I see. You just sit there and moan, don't you? Full of self-pity. You're rotten with it.

Neil (*standing up*) I'm not taking this from you.

Kath Poor little Nicky! You want to try thinking about someone else for a change.

(**Kath** *goes out.* **Neil** *sits down again*)

Scene 3

(*The same room. A short time later.* **Linda** *comes in*)

Linda Have you been sitting in the same place ever since I went out?

Neil If you've come back in that mood, you can save it.

Linda I've not come back in any mood. I just thought you might have cleared this place up.

Neil It's not my job.

Linda No. Nothing's your job, is it?

Neil Listen! I've had nothing but that kind of yap from the rest of your family all morning. If all you came back for is to be like that, you can clear off again.

Linda Can I? I've been working hard all morning and that's what I get. One of these days I might not come back at all.

Neil Where else could you go?

Linda I could go back to Mum and Dad. That's where. They'd have me.

Neil Feel free.

Linda I will. I'm serious, you know. I'm not going on like this.

Neil No? Well – neither am I. One of these days I might take off.

Linda Like Greg, eh?

Neil Yes. And like Bob Dent. They had enough of it. I might just move in with Greg.

Linda You'd be a right pair. You could booze together night and day, couldn't you?

Neil Oh, give it a rest.

Linda Where's Nicky?

Neil Upstairs. With your Mum and Kath.

Linda Why?

Neil She had an accident. They're looking after her.

Linda What accident?

Neil She fell off the shed roof.

Linda She what? Is she hurt? What were you doing?

Neil She's all right. I was in here. I didn't see her. It was an accident, I tell you.

Linda You're great, aren't you? Just great. You can't even look after a little kid properly.

Neil Yes. That's right. You're so dead right. I'm hopeless. Useless!

Linda Where are you going?

Neil Out.

Linda But it's dinnertime. When will you be back?

Neil You'll be lucky. The way I feel now – never!

(**Neil** *goes out*)

Scene 4

(*The same room. It is later in the afternoon.* **Kath, Linda** *and* **Mrs Banks** *are sitting together*)

Linda I wonder where he can have got to.

Kath It's my fault. I went on at him a bit.

Linda No. He's so touchy. When he was working we never had a cross word. Now we have nothing but quarrels all the time.

Mrs Banks Don't be silly. You did right to tell him off. Nicky could have been seriously hurt.

Kath Oh, come on, Mum. It was only a graze. She's been playing happily all afternoon.

Mrs Banks He's careless. Lazy.

Linda He's not lazy.

Mrs Banks I wish he was here. I'd give him a piece of my mind.

Kath That would do a lot of good, wouldn't it? He'd love that.

Mrs Banks Don't you be cheeky.

Linda I can't help wondering.

Kath About what?

Linda Well, you say things you don't mean. We were having a bit of a row. It was about nothing really, as usual. He said he was never coming back.

Mrs Banks He'll be back. He knows when he's well off, that one does.

Kath He probably went down to the White Swan.

Linda Don't say that. He's got most of the money with him.

Mrs Banks I can't stop any longer. I've got your Dad's tea to get ready. Are you coming, Kath?

Kath I'll be along in a minute.

Mrs Banks I'll see you both later, then. Give little Nicky a kiss from me.

Linda I will.

(**Mrs Banks** *goes out*)

Linda I'm worried, you know.

Kath So am I. I didn't like to say so in front of Mum.

Linda It's awful being unemployed. It's the boredom, having nothing to do all day.

Kath And feeling useless. It makes people spiteful.

(**Neil** *comes in*)

Linda Where have you been?

Neil Down town.

Kath With Greg?

Neil No. Not with Greg. Poor bloke's in trouble. I met Bob Dent. He told me.

Linda What sort of bother?

Neil Some lousy swine shopped them to the Social Security about that moonlighting they've been doing. Both Greg and Andy could be up in court for it.

Linda Oh dear!

Kath Look Neil – about this morning. I'm sorry. I spoke out of turn.

Neil No you didn't. I had it coming. It sank in, anyway.

Linda What were you doing down town?

Neil Walking about. Talking to people. I went to the College and the Careers Centre to look at some leaflets. I might start a course.

Kath I'd better go. I'm sorry for going on at you, Neil. I didn't mean it.

Neil That's all right, kid. How's Nicky?

Kath Oh, she was more frightened than hurt.

Neil Your mother didn't think so.

Linda Well you know what Mum's like.

Kath As soon as Nicky felt better, she was out playing again. She's having another little nap upstairs.

Linda I'd better get her up. Otherwise she won't sleep tonight. What's that you've got?

Neil Some seed packets.

Kath I'd better be off. If I hang about here too long, I'll cop it from Mum.

Linda Right, Kath. See you.

Kath Cheers, Neil. It is all right, isn't it?

Neil Of course it is.

Kath Good. 'Bye.

(**Kath** *goes out*)

Neil I'll pop up and see Nicky. (*At the door he turns back*) Look, love, I'm sorry for taking off like that.

Linda No. It was mostly my fault – and Mum's and Kath's. I heard all about it.

Neil It was me. Kath gave me a good telling off and she was right.

Linda She wasn't. It's rotten for you being out of work. I know.

Neil It's not the end of the world. I shouldn't let it get me down so much. As Kath said, I've got you and Nicky. That still means a lot to me though you mightn't think so the way I've been going on lately.

Linda I know. And you mean a lot to us. I don't know why we two are always rowing.

Neil We'll have to stop that.

Linda We must try. What are the seeds for?

Neil I didn't spend much. It was your Mum. She said I ought to grow some vegetables.

Linda Oh, you don't want to pay any attention to her.

Neil She could be right. I'll start digging up that back patch of ground tonight.

Linda You don't have to, love.

Neil I'll make a start. I'm going to do things. I've decided.. Anything's better than watching telly all day. Drives you mad.

Linda All right.

Neil I'll go and get Nicky up.

Linda She's all right for a bit. You put your feet up and I'll make you a cup of tea. You must be tired after all that walking about.

Neil No, I'm not. I feel different about things now. Better. I'll go up.

Linda I'm glad. I feel different, too. Come on, we'll go up and see to her together.

(*As they go out of the room,* **Neil** *puts his arm round* **Linda**)

People in the play

1 What are Neil's reasons for not joining Andy and Greg?
2 Why does he lie at first and say that Linda is out shopping?
3 Has he good reasons for not visiting the White Swan or is he being too sensitive? Say why you think as you do.
4 Of the three men, Neil, Andy and Greg, who is the most thick-skinned? Give some evidence from the play in your answer.

5 Is Neil a good father to Nicky or not? Give reasons for your answer.
6 Kath suggests to Neil that he should try going to the Stadium or the baths or the College. Is he sensible to turn down these suggestions, or is he just depressed and bad-tempered? Explain why you answer as you do.
7 Is Mrs Banks kind-hearted and understanding or not? In a few lines give your opinion of her, with some evidence from the play to support it.
8 Kath says that Neil is full of self-pity. Is she being fair or not? Say why you think as you do.
9 What can be said in Neil's defence when he rushes out of the house after his argument with Linda?
10 Why might Kath not want to go home with Mrs Banks?
11 When Neil comes back, Linda tells him to put his feet up while she makes him some tea. Is she being too soft-hearted, or kind and helpful? Explain why you think as you do.

On the dole

1 Andy and Greg, Kath and Mrs Banks all offer Neil help or advice. Which of them, do you think, is most sensible and helpful? Who is least sensible and helpful?
2 How much do you sympathise with Neil? Do your feelings about him change at the end of the play? Do you think his attitude has really changed for the better? Will he make more effort and be less wrapped up in himself in the future, or will he start feeling sorry for himself again?
3 If you were out of a job, with no hope of getting one, what could you find to do in your area that would help you to keep active? Which activities might you choose? If there aren't any, what sort of thing would you like there to be?

Writing

1 Mrs Banks seems to like telling people what to do. *Either*: Write the scene when she goes home to complain to her

husband about Neil and Mr Banks tries to defend him. Set it out like a play. *Or*: Write a scene in play form where Mrs Banks goes into a shop and is not satisfied with the service.

2 Write *either* an imaginary *or* a real account of what happened when you were left in charge of one or more children.

3 Andy and Greg have been working on a building site. An official interviews them about what they have been doing. What explanations do they give? Write the scene in play form.

4 Do you make a special effort to keep fit or do you feel that too much fuss is made about fitness these days? Write down your views on the subject. If you do something special to keep fit, describe what you do.

Hanging On

Bob
Frank
Len
Ted } *employees of Harry Jackson*
Alan
Alice
Enid
Harry Jackson
Anne, *his wife*
Sarah
Gavin } *his children*
Mr Warren
Jenny, *Harry Jackson's secretary*

Scene 1

(*A large group of workers are gathered together in the partitioned-off space in Harry Jackson's factory which serves as a canteen*)

Bob I wouldn't like to be in his shoes.
Enid We can't be getting many new orders.
Bob He looks worried sick.
Frank Don't worry about him. He'll be looking after himself. He's one of the boss class, isn't he?
Ted I wonder if he's going to lay some of us off.
Frank That could be it. Isn't it always the workers who have to make the sacrifices? If you're a boss, like Jackson, you can skate over hardships.

Enid I'll tell you one thing. I haven't seen him in that big Jag of his for months.

Len His wife's probably driving it.

Alice Toffee-nosed thing, she is. When she sees you in the street, she never speaks.

Alan He always comes to work in a Sierra now.

Ted My heart bleeds for him. He wants to try coming in to work on my motor-bike on a winter morning.

Frank If he's swopped his Jag for a Sierra, it'll be some kind of fiddle.

Ted Aye. Jackson's on the make, just like every other boss.

Alan I don't see that. Why didn't he stay down south? There's a lot more money there than there is up here.

Len Fat lot you know, lad. He'll have got a big government subsidy to start up a factory in this area.

Alice What kind of subsidy?

Frank The usual kind, Alice. A lot of money.

Alice Who told you?

Frank I don't need anyone to tell me. I can read the papers. They advertise these things.

Enid You're always on about those government subsidies, Frank. You don't know whether he got one or not. You never give Mr Jackson half a chance.

Ted Listen to her – 'Mr' Jackson.

Enid Oh, you shut your trap, Ted.

Alan He seems a decent kind of bloke to me.

Frank Who asked you, kid? You don't know anything yet. I've had years. Years. You're still wet behind the ears.

(**Harry Jackson** *comes in*)

Len Hey up! He's here.

Harry Afternoon. Thank you for agreeing to this meeting. I'll be as quick as I can.

Frank I bet he will. He doesn't want us late back to work.

Bob Shut up, Frank.

Harry You all know the firm's been doing very badly lately.

Ted It's not been our fault, Mr Jackson.

Harry I agree. As far as work and production go, you've done everything you could.

Ted We all enjoy the work here, Mr Jackson.

Harry Good. I only wish I could say with any confidence that it's going to go on.

Enid What do you mean?

Harry We're up against it. I've put all the money I had into the firm and borrowed as much as I could from the bank. Now our credit's run out. I'm going to have to close down.

Len Close down?

Enid When?

Harry I can pay everybody's wages for another two weeks.

Frank Why weren't we told this before?

Bob Come on, Frank. We knew things were going downhill.

Ted We didn't know it was that bad.

Enid Can't you go to the bank again, Mr Jackson? Ask them to tide us over?

Harry Don't you think I've done that? I've done everything except go down on my bended knees. I'd have done that, too, if I'd thought it would do any good.

Alan So that's it, then. Two weeks.

Harry Not quite. We can take a gamble.

Alice What sort of gamble?

Harry There's just a chance that we might get a German order and one from Bristol in the next four weeks. With those the bank might think again and see us through.

Bob Four weeks is too late. We'll all be on the dole by then.

Harry If you all agreed to go on half time, we could keep going for four weeks.

Len Half time?

Frank Half pay.

Ted And what happens after four weeks?

Harry I don't know. We trust to luck.

Frank So we go on half pay for four weeks just on an off-chance.

Harry You can put it like that. You'd only be working half time.

Enid It's a bit of a shock.

Harry I'm doing the best I can. If the firm closes, I stand to lose most of the money I've put in. But you lose your jobs. We're all in it together.

Bob How much hope is there of getting these orders?

Harry I just don't know. You can work for two more weeks on full pay, of course. It's up to you. You could be looking for other jobs during that time.

Ted There aren't any other jobs.

Alice My Joe's been out of work for nearly a year.

Alan I wouldn't be getting much more than I could draw on the dole.

Harry I'm not asking you to decide this minute. Talk about it – here and at home. I'll meet you all here again tomorrow at the same time. You can give me your answer then. Good afternoon.

(**Harry** *goes out*)

Frank It's a liberty. He should have warned us before that things were so bad.

Bob How would that have helped?

Ted We could have been looking for other work.

Enid Don't be daft. Where?

Len I'd rather be on half time for four weeks with a chance of work than on full time for two with no hope.

Alice I'm going to take half time. I've got to.

Enid Money's short enough at home as it is.

Len I was out of work for six months before I came here.

Alan We'd better go for half time.

Frank That's not for you to say, my lad. We'll have to vote on it.

Bob But not now. We'll do as he says – talk it over and vote tomorrow.

Ted How about doing that at tea-break in the morning?

Frank Right.

Enid Come on, Alice. Let's get back to work.

Len I don't know what the wife will say.

(*They all begin to move back to work*)

Scene 2

(*Harry Jackson's house. About a week later.* **Anne, Sarah** *and* **Gavin** *are together.* **Harry** *comes in*)

Anne You were a long time. You did see the doctor, didn't you?

Harry Yes. He says there's nothing seriously wrong with me. Just worry.

Anne I told you so. That business of yours is just too much for you.

Harry Maybe.

Anne I always said it was a stupid idea to set up your factory in this part of the country. Crazy. Everything's just gone downhill for us.

Gavin Yes. Why can't we go back down south? I hate that lousy school. They're always making fun of the way I talk.

Sarah You can't even afford to let us go away on holiday.

Harry A holiday? We'll be lucky to have even a roof over our heads, the way things are going.

Anne That's silly talk.

Harry Is it? You know that second mortgage I took out on the house?

Anne What about it?

Harry The bank want their money back.

Anne But they can't! They can't make us sell the house!

Harry Can't they? We might have to.

Anne Harry! How could you be so stupid! What are we going to do?

Sarah Dad! Where are we going to live?

Harry Don't worry. I was exaggerating. We'll pull through.

Gavin Can't you sell the firm, Dad?

Harry Only at a big loss.

Anne But if we're in danger of losing the house, we're going to lose everything. You'll have to sell the firm.

Harry We've got to hang on.

Anne Hang on? For Heaven's sake – why?

Harry Well, for one thing a lot of people depend on the firm for their jobs.

Anne Don't be stupid! You can't think about the workers. You've got to think about us.

Harry I do think about you. But I owe them something.

Anne Don't be a fool! What do you owe them? It's your firm –

your money. They wouldn't give you a second thought if they were in your place. Lazy, idle lot!

Harry Be fair, Anne.

Anne You're the one who's not being fair. Think of your family. The workers! It's all their fault that you're in difficulty. They've no loyalty to the firm.

Harry They've got some. They agreed a week ago to go on half time to keep us in business.

Anne For how long?

Harry Who knows? About another three weeks for certain.

Sarah Three weeks!

Anne You'll have to sell up. You'll have to!

Harry Listen! All our money's in the firm along with a bank loan. Then I took a second mortgage and sold the Jaguar. The firm's swallowed that up. There's no way of getting much of it back by selling out now.

Anne This is terrible, Harry! What are we going to do?

Harry Hope and pray. Just now I'm going to write some letters.

(**Harry** *starts to go*)

Gavin Oh! I forgot.

Harry What?

Gavin A Mr Warren rang. He'd like to call at the factory and see you sometime. He wants you to ring him back tonight.

Harry What's his number?

Gavin It's on the pad by the phone.

Harry Right.

(**Harry** *goes out*)

Scene 3

(*Harry's office at the factory. A few days later.* **Harry** *is at his desk.* **Jenny** *comes in*)

Jenny There's a Mr Warren to see you, Mr Jackson.

Harry He's early. Show him in.

Jenny (*through the door*) Come in, please.

(**Mr Warren** *comes in*)

Mr Warren Morning, Mr Jackson. How are things?

Harry Oh, not too bad, Mr Warren. Not too bad at all.

Mr Warren I see. Well, you know what I've come about?

Harry I can make a good guess. Do sit down. Would you like some coffee?

Mr Warren No, thanks. This won't take long. As I said over the phone, I heard you might be in the market.

Harry Yes. I could be.

Mr Warren I'm prepared to make you an offer for the premises.

Harry You mean the business.

Mr Warren No, I don't. I'm not interested in your machinery or stock. I just want to take over the buildings – the factory and offices.

Harry Now, wait a bit. The business is worth a lot more than just the buildings.

Mr Warren Maybe and maybe not. It certainly isn't to me. I want the buildings for warehouse space. I'm not interested in the rest of the business.

Harry And how about the people working here?

Mr Warren They'd have to go. I've got my own staff.

Harry And the machinery – the stock?

Mr Warren You'd have to sell that elsewhere. I'm only interested in the buildings – empty.

Harry I got the impression over the phone that you were interested in buying more than just those.

Mr Warren No.

Harry I see. What sort of price were you thinking of offering then?

Mr Warren That would take a bit of discussion.

Harry I'm not going to give the place away, you know.

Mr Warren No. But it's up to you now.

Harry I'll have to consider it.

Mr Warren You do that. The girl has my card and phone number. I'll wait to hear from you. Good morning.

Harry Good morning.

(**Mr Warren** *goes out*)

Scene 4

(The Jacksons' house. The same evening. The family are sitting together)

Anne You've been very quiet. Are things getting worse?
Harry I've had an offer.
Sarah For the firm?
Gavin Oh – take it!
Anne What a relief!
Harry Relief? I don't know about that. It's a Mr Warren. He just wants to buy the buildings.
Sarah Still – that's something.
Harry Is it? Those buildings are only a fraction of the real value of the whole business. And even at that he's hoping to get them dirt cheap.
Anne Oh, Harry – what a mess!
Harry I'll have to start right at the beginning again. I'll have to find a job.
Gavin But we could move back down south, couldn't we?
Sarah We could have a holiday this year after all.
Anne And a better car. There must be a bright side.
Harry Must there? When I've settled all the debts, we'd probably have just enough left to pay off that second mortgage.
Anne But we wouldn't lose the house.
Harry That's about all we'd be able to keep – if that. We'd be back just where we were seventeen or eighteen years ago. Right at the bottom of the ladder again.
Gavin Go on, Dad. Sell up.
Anne Are you going to?
Harry I'm going to have to. But it means we'll all be out of work.

Scene 5

(**Harry's** *office.* **Harry** *is looking at an order sheet.* **Jenny** *is standing by his desk. It is about a week later*)

Jenny Is it a good order, Mr Jackson?

Harry (*throws the order sheet on his desk*) It's maddening, Jenny. That's what it is.

Jenny How do you mean, Mr Jackson?

Harry It's the one from that firm in Bristol. I've been hanging on for it and hanging on, hoping it might save us. But it's just not big enough. I'll have to write to Bristol to say that we can't take their order as we're having to close down.

Jenny How soon, Mr Jackson?

Harry Ten days – maybe a fortnight. I'll have to tell the others this lunchtime.

Jenny Well, we were warned. But it's rotten just the same.

Harry It's damned bad luck, Jenny. Heartbreaking.

Jenny I'm very sorry.

Harry So am I. For everybody. The workforce – they stood by the business. I don't know how I'm going to tell them.

Jenny It's not your fault.

Harry Maybe not. It doesn't make it any easier. Oh – I'm in no mood for writing to Bristol. I just want to get it over. Have you got that card from Mr Warren handy?

Jenny Yes. In my office.

Harry I'd better see if he's still interested. Get him for me, will you? Put him through when he's on the line.

Jenny Yes, Mr Jackson.

(**Jenny** *goes out.* **Harry** *sits at his desk and gloomily looks at the order sheet. The phone rings*)

Harry Hello! Is that Mr Warren? (*Pause*) Sorry, it's a bad line. Mr Warren? (*Pause*) Germany? Mr Reinhold? What? (*A longer pause*) How much? Good grief! Say that again. (*A long pause*) Wait! Wait! Just let me get hold of a pen to take all the figures down. (*Gets a pen*) Right. Go on. (*A long pause while he is writing with the phone at his ear*) Yes. (*Pause*) Yes. That's fantastic! Marvellous! (*Pause*) In the post already? Good. Great. Terrific. Thanks. Thanks a lot, Klaus. Goodbye. (*He stands up*) Jenny! Jenny!

(**Jenny** *comes in*)

Jenny I'm sorry. That German call came through just as I went back into the office. Shall I get Mr Warren now?

Harry Blow Mr Warren! Forget him. Do you know who that was, Jenny?

Jenny Our German agent.

Harry Right. He's got us a big order – an enormous order, at a good price. I'm going out. Hold the fort.

Jenny When will you be back?

Harry Soon, I hope. I'm going down to the bank. With these figures to show him, I'm sure I can talk Hudson into extending our loan. Forget all I said, Jenny. We're still in business!

Scene 6

(*As in Scene 1, the canteen.* **Harry** *is just finishing his talk to the workforce*)

Harry So, to sum up, we have orders to keep us going for three months. The bank has agreed to give us more credit. We're back to normal.

Bob Three months?

Harry It's a lot longer than I hoped for at one time.

Len Better than two weeks.

Enid Maybe business is going to pick up all round.

Harry Maybe. Anyway, that's all I had to say. I thought you'd be pleased to hear it. And thanks again for standing by the firm.

(**Harry** *goes out*)

Bob What a relief.

Len The wife'll be tickled pink to hear it.

Alice He's a clever man is Mr Jackson to bring us through.

Frank Clever? I'll bet he was just lucky.

Enid You never have a good word for anyone, Frank, do you?

Alan He was the one who kept us going, anyway.

Frank Don't you believe it. We kept things going by agreeing to work half time.

Ted That's right. Really speaking, we've given up two weeks' pay.

Frank And we'll never see that again.

Enid How do you know? He did say something about bonuses.

Alan Yes, he did.

Frank Bonuses? Pigs might fly. Catch a boss giving anything he doesn't have to give to his workers.

Ted He only said it because he was feeling good. He'll have come out of this okay.

Frank He'll have made something. It certainly won't have cost him anything. Only us.

Ted You can say that again, Frank. We paid the price. It's always the workers who make the sacrifices. Bosses, like Jackson, don't know they're born.

People in the play

1 From Scene 1, giving some reasons for your answer, name two characters who seem fairly sympathetic towards Harry Jackson.

2 From the same scene, again giving your reasons, name two characters who seem opposed to him.

3 How do you know, from Scene 1, that Mrs Jackson is not at all interested in the workers at the factory?

4 Which of the workers in that scene tries to influence the others and seems to want to be the leader?

5 Alice says that she has 'got to' go on half time. Why might she have to do that? What is her husband doing?

6 Why might Len be the quickest to agree to go on half time?

7 In Scene 2 Gavin says he wants to go back south again. Is his reason a good one or not? Say why you think as you do.

8 In Scene 3 why might Harry Jackson pretend to Mr Warren that the business is not doing badly?

9 In Scene 4 why is Sarah pleased when she hears about the offer for the firm?

10 Name two characters in Scene 6 who are pleased with what Harry Jackson has done, and give reasons for your answer.

11 Name two characters in Scene 6 who have not changed their attitude towards Harry Jackson, and give reasons for your answer.

12 Has any worker changed his or her attitude towards Harry Jackson by the end of the play or not? Say why you think as you do.

Workers and management

1 Do you approve of the attitude of Harry Jackson's family? Is he wrong not to have considered them more? Or do you think they are selfish and should have given him more support?

2 In Scene 2 Harry says he 'owes' the workers a chance of a job. His wife disagrees, saying they have 'no loyalty'. Is she right? Are they staying with the firm because there are no jobs elsewhere? Or are you more in agreement with Harry?

Writing

1 How does Harry Jackson's family react when he tells them he is not going to sell the business after all? Are they disappointed or does he manage to convince them it is the only sensible thing to do? Write the scene between him, his wife and the two children in play form.

2 When Len has to go home and tell his wife they are going on half time, he is worried about what she will say. Is this because she has had to give up her job through illness? Perhaps she is having a baby and they are short of money as it is. Or is she rather a difficult and bad-tempered woman? Write in play form the scene when Len goes home and tells her.

3 If you were producing this play you would have to pick people who looked right for their parts. You would have to think about their ages, how they moved about and how they spoke as well as how they might be dressed. Pick one of the characters and describe what you think he or she might look like and how he or she might speak and behave.